1998 For

From Mary Kay
&
Alex

The Optimist's Guide

To Everyday Living

By Sophia and Jesse Bedford-Pierce

Illustrated by Paul Brent

Designed by Arlene Greco

PETER PAUPER PRESS, INC.
WHITE PLAINS, NEW YORK

For Linner, Totie, and Bear for looking on the bright side.

Illustrations copyright © 1998 Paul Brent

Text copyright © 1998
Peter Pauper Press, Inc.
202 Mamaroneck Avenue
White Plains, NY 10601
All rights reserved
ISBN 0-88088-069-4
Printed in China
7 6 5 4 3 2 1

The Optimist's Guide
To Everyday Living

Contents

Introduction

*Keep your face to the sunshine and
you cannot see the shadow.*

—HELEN KELLER

*In the time when Dendid created
    all things,
He created the sun,
And the sun is born, and dies,
    and comes again.*

—OLD AFRICAN SONG OF *DINKA* ORIGIN

The optimist believes that self-confidence and trust are the bedrock of
things that are worth building. The
optimist believes embracing that
which is worthwhile creates an inner

feeling of creativity and well-being. The optimist is also aware that the rock of confidence is subject to wear and tear by the elements, that we often face unpredictable difficulties, and that not everything is "fair."

Some people inherently know that things will become better, that positive thoughts result in positive actions. But don't confuse optimism with naiveté. Most of us have to learn how to tap into optimism in a world that can often be harsh.

This journey in book form offers insights into happiness, a pathway to joy, a world-view that makes us become stronger with each day. It is a journey offered in stories and wise words that has served us well and will make you feel at *your* optimum as you adopt the optimist's mode.

Praise the Earth

There's a tree that grows in Brooklyn. Some people call it the Tree of Heaven. No matter where its seed falls, it makes a tree which struggles to reach the sky.

—BETTY SMITH,
A TREE GROWS IN BROOKLYN

Perseverance is a great element of success. If you only knock long enough and loud enough at the gate, you are sure to wake up somebody.

—HENRY WADSWORTH LONGFELLOW

My grandfather Bo was born and raised on a piece of land that other local farmers characterized as having "two stones for every dirt." That Bo's father, and his father before him, had made any kind of living on that property was an amazement and an amusement to their neighbors. Bo's father told him how he watched his own father struggle to repair an inordinate number of broken plow blades, rebuild after heavy floods, and try to put together enough money for a new season's seed after too many meager harvests, even as he himself wearied through the same cycle.

As a young man Bo earned a scholarship to a state college to study modern agricultural methods. He returned from school each summer ever more aware that even with new techniques the farm would continue to produce less and less in the way of salable harvests. Bo was saddened to see his father's resources and resolve diminish. As he prepared to finish his last year of studies, Bo made a promise to himself that he would find a way to save the family farm. After graduation he implemented as many improvements as he could, but the soil would not grow enough of a crop to make ends meet.

One afternoon after Sunday supper Bo's father told him, in a manner as

calm and clear as the water in the
pond, that he didn't see any way to
avoid putting the farm up for sale. My
grandfather Bo began to protest. He
could barely control his anger at their
circumstance, and began to curse the
ground that had been his family's
homestead. His father looked at Bo
sternly and said:

Whatever befalls us don't curse
the earth, or the stones, or belit-
tle the flowers that find their
way between them. For without
the seed that preceded them
even they would not be here,
nor without the seed that preceded us would we. What we
have had is what we have had.

Be thankful for it as I am, and as
my father was before us.

My grandfather Bo left the table and
went out to the ruined fields and
kicked at the ground. When he
calmed down just enough to look up,
the afternoon light illuminated a
patch of wildflowers—purples and
blues, reds and whites, mingling in
nature's bouquet. They afforded a
dramatic contrast to the pile of large
flat stones that had been moved out
of the way.

Grandfather Bo harvested the seed of
those wildflowers. He cleaned and
sorted them. He measured them by
weight and placed them in small

packets printed with colorful illustrations of the flowers in bloom. Some seed he set aside to replant. The next season he repeated what he had done and added other desirable wildflowers that would take to his soil. He harvested the seed of the new Spring's bounty and sold more packets. In time he had found so many varieties that would thrive on the farm that he created a catalog to sell the seed.

Bo's prosperity grew with his flowers. The local farmers remain amazed to this day, but very few of them remain amused. Bo had looked to himself and to the earth for sustenance, and he had been rewarded.

What Is Lovely
Never Dies

*What really matters is what you do
with what you have.*

—Shirley Lord

*We have two or three great and moving experiences in our lives . . . We
tell our two or three stories—each
time in a new disguise—maybe ten
times, maybe a hundred, as long as
people will listen.*

—F. Scott Fitzgerald

*What is lovely never dies, but passes
into other loveliness, star-dust or
sea-foam, flower or winged air.*

—Thomas Bailey Aldrich

Grandpa characterized my grand-
mother Sadie as a woman who
believed that goodness engendered
goodness, that kindness ultimately
returned in kind, and that it was
important to make the best possible
day out of every day. I had always
accepted Grandpa's and my mother's word for this description of
Sadie, who passed away before I was
born and before my mother had
reached adulthood.

On the morning of my twenty-first
birthday my mother handed me a
wrapped box that, although
unopened, seemed somehow aged.
In the box was a bound journal
with the inscription: "For my grand-

daughter, as yet unborn, for the day
that she comes of age," and it said:

> Dearest granddaughter:
> Although it is unlikely that we
> will meet in this earthly life, I
> am writing down my random
> thoughts (and occasional admo-
> nitions) in the hope that when
> you receive this journal you will
> find the things I would have
> said to you of pleasure, and
> perhaps of some practical use.

I was transfixed. I was amazed. I
savored the resonance of Grandma's
words, spoken in a voice that I could
only imagine. I was struck by the
truth of how Grandpa and Mother
had described Sadie. Here I could

have my own conversation with a woman whose optimism about life transcended the earthly time that she had called her own.

I often return to her journal, reading favorite passages, trying to imagine where Grandma had been sitting or what she had been wearing when she wrote a particular entry. As I recall Grandma's words and ruminate on her example, I remind myself that goodness is a gift, kindness is a way of being, and it is always worth the extra effort to try to make something meaningful from everything I do.

A Beacon for
All to See

*They can do all because they think
they can.*

—Virgil

Power is the ability to make change.

—Geneva Overholser

*I have often thought that the people
who built lighthouses, and those who
kept them, were optimists. A lighthouse is a beacon to all on the sea—
a sure sign that land is near and
that someone aloft is keeping a
steadfast eye for their safe passage.*

—Fletcher Cairns

For several childhood summers we vacationed on a section of the Cape known as Highpoint Light. Our friend Bud Hermann was, in season, a naturalist on a whale-watching ship that plied the waters guarded by that lighthouse. Bud made his livelihood in the same waters that his ancestors sailed, although they had intended a very different fate for the whales that they tracked. Bud's search for ocean life required a mixture of scientific knowledge and tenacity, and no small measure of optimism. The towns-people and the summer people alike thought of Bud as an outgoing man. Few, however, were prepared for the intensity of his response when a coastal engineer projected that the promontory on which the lighthouse was situated would erode at a rate that would send it into the ebb and flow of the sea within five years.

Bud came forward with a plan that had some among his neighbors believing that the salt air had finally penetrated the inner workings of his mind. "This lighthouse which has long served us is imperiled," said Bud. "There is not one among us who could safely go about his business without its watchful beacon. It is clear to me that we have to move the lighthouse back 400 feet. I am told that this will keep it from harm's way for at least the next 100 years."

The estimates for lifting, relocating, refurbishing and reanchoring the lighthouse far exceeded the means of the local municipality. Inquiries to state and federal agencies made it apparent that substantial private funds would have to be secured.

Bud created a "move the lighthouse" foundation. He convinced the local park service to let volunteers bring in a trailer near the light to sell souvenirs. He went to the local schools and enlisted the students to collect the refunds from empty bottles. He commissioned artisans to create crafts for sale that used Highpoint Light as a motif. He used every opportunity to encourage donations. All of this money went to the cause. In one of life's (not so small) miracles, after exactly three years to the day, the lighthouse foundation had raised sufficient funds to undertake and complete the task.

We take our own children to the Cape now. We often go to Highpoint Light to watch its beacon sweep across the shore and sea. We take special pleasure in pointing to a rock with a thin steel pole emerging from it, as it is washed over by the waves. And we tell our children—to their amazement—that, if not for the insistent vision of one Bud Hermann, that is where the lighthouse would now be.

Look Well
to This Day

Yesterday is but a dream, tomorrow is but a vision. But today well lived makes every yesterday a dream of happiness and every tomorrow a vision of hope. Look well, therefore, to this day.

—Sanskrit proverb

To live is so startling it leaves little time for anything else.

—Emily Dickinson

You really can change the world if you care enough.

—Marian Wright Edelman

"Our town had been a beautiful place with lively sounds, and an abundance of food," Mother told me. "But the time of prosperity ended when the wild winds came across the plains and decimated the land. The storms did not abate for weeks. The people in the capital had no compassion for us. They kept what was available in the way of medicine and food rations for themselves, or diverted it for their own gain." Mother told me of a time after the season of the winds when the talk at the site of what had been the market became mournful, and after a time even the mournful sounds gave way to silence. There was no flour for bread, and little grew in the fields.

Mother continued, "Your father and I splintered our furniture and burned it for heat to get through the winter. Fresh water was scarce. We gave only occasional thought to how our clothing appeared or if our faces were clean. I would run a brush through my hair before the bristles became too loose to be useful, but soon the bristles were rubbed into nubs and I burned the brush too." I could not believe what I was hearing. The town was not now this dark place that mother described. It resembled exactly what she told me of the prosperous times. "Mother, have you had a bad dream?" I asked. "How can the town that you describe have been so bleak? And if what you tell me is true, how has our town and our home returned to its former abundance?"

"Everything that I've told you is true, Jessica. The resurrection of this place is a miracle. And the spirit of renewed hope and optimism emerged because of you and your friends." Now I truly thought that Mother had gone mad. "Mother," I said, "I don't understand. I have no memory of these bad times. My friends and I are children. We couldn't have done anything to change the devastation that you describe."

"One night," Mother continued, "we heard rumbling. We thought that it

was another series of storms. But the rumbling was the sound of heavy vehicles. When the sound of the vehicles ground down, we heard, to our amazement, the sounds of babies. The vehicles were filled with tiny babies wrapped in blankets. The nurses who drove this caravan explained that in their town the storms had hit with full force when the adults and the older children were in a meeting house.

The babies had been in the nursery in the care of a few nurses and child minders. The meeting house and all who were in it had been swept away. But the nursery stood behind a great rock wall. This natural shelter had protected the infants and the few adults who were watching them. These babies were now without parents or older siblings to care for them. These few women did not have the means to feed and house so many babies. So they had set out to find people who would care for the infants.

The elders of our town tried to explain that we had little and that, despite a desire to show compassion, we could do little. The woman leading the caravan simply responded, "you may have little, but these babies are alone, and have less than little. In truth these babies have nothing."

"And you, Jessica, were one of those babies."

Where Will It Lead, and Where Did It Start?

We don't know who we are until we see what we can do.

—MARTHA GRIMES

Out of each experience enough light is generated to illuminate another little stretch. Who knows where it will lead? And who can tell where it started?

—CESAR CHAVEZ

If I am not for myself, who will be for me? But if I am for myself only, what am I? And if not now, when?

—HILLEL

The day had not started well. The alarm clock didn't ring. Or if it rang I reflexively turned it off and went back to sleep. By the time I was awakened I had precious few minutes to wash and dress, and of course no time to give breakfast a look. I missed the bus, waited for the next one, and was too late for the train I had originally planned to take. I finally seated myself on the train headed toward work, but I was feeling breathless and stressed. As I made the effort to regain my composure, I realized that I had left my paper work on the desk at home and had not put it back into my case. I looked inside the case hoping to find what I needed, but I had to acknowledge that my case was empty. I scanned the faces of other passengers, looked at my shoes, looked up at the ceiling and out the window at the passing blur, and lowered my eyes to look back at my shoes again.

A moan and then a scream came from the back of the car several rows behind me.

"Someone's fainted," shouted one passenger. "This lady's real sick," called another voice. "Conductor, conductor, get the conductor" was heard from several directions. "Is anyone here a doctor?" asked a girl in a green coat. I was thinking so fast that

I wasn't thinking at all. I ran to where a woman with ashen skin was lying on the floor.

I am not a doctor and my emergency skills are probably average or less, but I knew at that moment that it was imperative to help the stricken woman regain consciousness. I coaxed and massaged her, I cajoled and comforted her. I kept asking her name, trying to reach her level of response. I rifled her purse to find a license with her photograph and name on it. "Come, Clara, come on out of it, Clara," I said. Her eyelids flickered, a breath emerged from her mouth. She mumbled with just enough clarity for me to imagine that she had said "my medicine, medicine." I looked through her purse again and found a prescription bottle in the name of Clara Weeks. I made her sit up a bit, placed a small tablet from the bottle on her tongue, and helped her sip from the cup of water that had been handed to me.

The train had made an emergency stop at a local station. The EMS crew boarded the train and parted the onlookers. A woman in a uniform told me that she'd "take over from here." Clara was carried to an ambulance of whose flashing red bubble light I had just become aware. As I returned to my seat I

P. Brent

felt pats on my back, and heard "great job," "quick thinking," "good work," and one tongue-in-cheek "you can save me anytime."

The conductor interviewed me and the other passengers. He wrote down names and times. He gave me a very hearty "Thanks for your help." The train pulled into Central Station and I walked across town to work. I thought that doing what I ordinarily do for the rest of that day would be an anticlimax. I realized very quickly, however, that doing what I do well and doing it with an awareness of its effect on others now held a new richness for me.

I try to incorporate that insight into my daily outlook and remember how special life is. Often, I like to re-read a note that I received several days later, on pale peach paper, that ends in a beautifully scripted, *Thank You.*

Infinite Possibilities

Along the way you will stumble, and perhaps even fall; but that, too, is normal and to be expected. Get up, get back on your feet, chastened but wiser, and continue on down the road.

—ARTHUR ASHE

Go behind the apparent circumstances of the situation and locate the love in yourself and in all others involved in the situation.

—MOTHER TERESA

I like to think of myself as an artist, and my life as my greatest work of art. Every moment is a moment of creation, and each moment of creation contains infinite possibilities.

—SHAKTI GAWAIN

Sophia rose in the morning like a vision from the East, lit by a wash of purple blue light gradually warming, as she emerged from her bed to full standing. She unfolded from her layers of sleep, finding pleasure in each movement of her body—as she had every morning since the day that she had come to the garden.

Sophia had come to the garden to paint it in its fullness. She had come with a mind to paint the broad sweep of the landscape, to follow the shadows shifting, the details altering as the light played its repertoire of variations. She had come to find a sheltered spot from which to observe the weather moving through this domain

in calm or in drama. Sophia had
come knowing that her palette would
evolve with colors of the seasons, and
of the seasons within the seasons.
She could not know when she first
entered there that the subject that
would most test her skills was not
the verdant garden. She could not
know what would push her to render
and paint with the full stroke of her
virtuosity.

Sophia had taken this commission
after completing her apprenticeship.
Arriving at the garden before winter
receded gave her time to become
familiar with its underlying forms.
She watched herself awaken within
the sheltering walls of the amber-

hued estate, and turn to see the frosty breath of morning like a white gauze on the window glass. She walked across the thin-planked floor to her dressing table. Sophia dabbed water on her eyelids, rubbed her cheeks, looked into the mirror, and wetted her eyes again. She dried herself with the towel that she had folded and laid on the radiator the night before. She stretched her limbs to put on a loose-fitting wheat-colored blouse, black leggings, and soft-topped black shoes. She brushed her hair with long strokes before tying it back just above the single-banded collar of her blouse.

Sophia placed the previous day's

sketches in her art bag, closed her hand around the handle of the paint box, exited her room, and descended the steps to the entry parlor of the house. She took notice of the tea that Mrs. Zinn had put out for her, but let it rest on the tray. She left the house to return to the grove where she had been sketching the day before.

In order to gain a new perspective she climbed the branches of a bare tree with her sketch pad in hand. Her pencils swung while tied with string to her belt loops so that they would not, as she changed pencils, be able to fall. In a moment of rapturous cre-ation, she forgot where she was perched and tumbled without grace to the ground.

Two of the gardeners who had heard her shriek, and the ensuing thud, came quickly to her aid. She could not stand.

The next morning Sophia awoke slowly, and felt as if a cloud had settled in her head. Mrs. Zinn was at her bedside. "Do not try to stand, Sophia," cautioned Mrs. Zinn. "Both of your legs were broken in the fall. You have a lengthy convalescence ahead of you." During the next few days Sophia regained clarity of mind. She asked the doctor, who came regularly, if she might begin to sketch again. The doctor thought it would

be a good way for her to fill the time. Even though she was allowed to sketch and read Sophia was not accustomed to long periods of inactivity, and her own self-pity seemed to be slowing her recovery. Mrs. Zinn sensed Sophia's frustration. "Sophia," said Mrs. Zinn, "there is a very young lady here at the house whom you have not met. The doctor has agreed to have you lifted into a wheelchair so that you may visit with her."

Sophia was puzzled but agreed to call on her. She was not prepared for the bright green eyes, the genuine smile, and the loving demeanor on the face of the young girl whose body had betrayed her since birth. Felicity had been stricken in a way that made it all but certain that she would never be mobile. Great efforts were made to move her onto the porch and to take her for short visits on the estate, but most of her time was spent indoors, usually in her own room where various machines helped her body do what it could not do for itself.

After several hours in Felicity's company, Sophia had regained some perspective on her own temporary condition. She asked to spend time with Felicity the next day, and the day after. She asked Mrs. Zinn if she might, while still convalescing, paint

the walls in Felicity's room. She
thought perhaps she could bring
some of the world outside into
Felicity's interior life. Mrs. Zinn
thought well of the idea and cleared
it with the doctor.

From the wheelchair Sophia began to
paint deserts, plains, forest floors,
and other land. She added nearby
ponds, and rushing water. When
Sophia could stand with support, she
painted the trees and portions of the
horizon line. As the weeks passed
and Sophia was fully mobile again,
she did not immediately return to the
garden. She walked back to Felicity's
room and, standing on a ladder,
painted agile birds, moving clouds,

and a sunlit sky illuminating the festive colors of a hundred hot air balloons.

The enchanting walls that Sophia painted created new horizons not only for Felicity, but for Sophia herself.